CW01024323

THE CTHULI

Developed by
PAUL BALDOWSKI

Made using **The Black Hack** (v1), created by David Black

Cover illustration: Cthulhu by Henning Ludvigsen
Copyright © 2008 - 2017 - www.henningludvigsen.com
Interior Illustrations: Karol Patola | Copyright © 2017 - jekjekyll.deviantart.com
Cthulhu icon by Studio Fibonacci from the Noun Project

Thanks to Richard August, Simon Taylor, Graham Spearing, Freddie Foulds, John Almack, Neil Benson

What's "The Cthulhu Hack"?

The Cthulhu Hack is a traditional tabletop role playing game. Friends sit around a table – or meet online – and narrate stories; as the Player, who acts the part of a character in the story, or as the **Gamemaster** (GM), who sets the scene, leads the tale, plays the part of non-player characters, and keeps order.

The balance might seem heavily weighted on the GM in work terms, but it's all about the story and having fun. The group around the table should always make the game entertaining for everyone.

The Cthulhu Hack core rules offer you a set of simple mechanics to run intriguing investigations, using concepts and creatures created by the author **H. P. Lovecraft**. What's more, the way the game works places the focus on the players - who roll all the dice and keep track of their various resources - to allow the GM to focus on fleshing out the world.

The **Players** are Investigators of the Unknown; ordinary people who, through curiosity, inheritance, or circumstance, have found themselves entangled in a tale of Cosmic Horror. Players imagine the world from their Investigator's viewpoint. When an Investigator tries to discover a clue, or fight for their life, the Player rolls a die to see if they succeed, or else to discover the consequences of their failure.

The **Gamemaster** prepares and presents the setup for the story. They describe the sensations of the wider world, the supporting characters, and the challenges. They fill in the details when Investigators use their senses or ask questions about events. The GM listens to what the Players say and works with them to create an exciting story, often using the Player's own vivid imaginations against them.

Seeds of Investigation

The footer of this book contains cryptic notes. I based these upon notes from Lovecraft's commonplace book; he jotted down hundreds of ideas for stories - some that he completed, others never started. Should you find yourself at a loose end for an adventure seed or something to mix up the action, flip to a random page.

The Core Mechanics

Two core mechanics drive the game - **Saves** and **Resources**. Both involve the Player making a dice roll. The game requires a full set of polyhedral dice, common to most tabletop role-playing games, ranging from 4-sided dice up to 20-sided.

When a **Threat** sets out to hamper or hurt an Investigator, the Player of that character rolls to Save them.

When an Investigator uses something to support or aid their progress, the Player rolls to check their **Resources** to see if they've pushed too far or run out of supplies.

Saves

A **Threat** is anything the GM uses against the Investigators to either hurt them or to hinder their progress. That could mean a zombie clawing their flesh, a rival trying to drug them, or a trap set to deter or hold intruders.

Investigators have six **Save** scores; each of which provides a means to resist a different kind of Threat. The GM sets which Save works against what Threat and the Player rolls a 20-sided die to resolve.

Check the character sheet at the end of this book to see examples of the sort of Threats that an Investigator might face. For example:

- *To fend off a zombie's grappling attack, you roll a Strength Save.*
- *To escape the iron jaws of a hidden trap, you roll a Dexterity Save.*
- *To resist a hypnotist's influence, you roll a Charisma Save.*

A situation should only require a Save if a clear threat exists – and the GM should clearly explain what consequences arise from both success and failure of the roll.

If the player **rolls under** their Save score, they succeed; they hurt their opponent or avoid whatever threatened them.

If they roll **equal or higher** than their **Save**, the Investigator has become hurt or hampered.

If they get hit, they lose **Hit Points** (see p 17). If a character loses all those points they're **Out of Action** (see p 17) - unconscious or too hurt to act - until someone provides first aid or can get the Investigator to a hospital.

If the **Threat** hinders or hampers, the GM describes a disastrous delay or complication that slows the character's progress toward their goal; the GM explains how the enemy gains the upper hand and acquires the rare artefact, or what traps the

Investigator forcing them to come up with a plan to escape.

Resources

Investigators use up **Resources** in three ways - **Supplies**, **Sanity**, and **Investigation**.

Instead of keeping track of individual resources, an Investigator rolls a die to see if they're getting low or if they've run out of something. Each **Resource** has a set size of die and you roll when the GM asks you to.

You always check your Resources after using them. So, you shoot your gun, find a clue, or witness something horrible. Then you roll. See the **Example of Play**, p 48.

If you roll a 1 or 2 on your Resource Die, the die steps down - if you rolled a 6-sided die and got a 1 or 2, next time you roll a 4-sided die. If you roll 1 or 2 on a 4-sided, that Resource ran out.

For **Sanity**, that means permanent madness. It's also worth noting that each time you roll 1 or 2 on any test of Sanity, the character suffers a bout of temporary insanity (see more about **Insanity** and **Shock**, p 26 / 28)

For **Investigation**, that means running out of options; your Investigator can't

progress without help from friends or falling back to recuperate (see p 6).

For **Supplies**, they're spent, broken, or lost – your gun clicks on empty, your torchlight gutters out, or you chow down on the last hardtack in the emergency rations.

Supplies

Investigators can easily lose track of their **Supplies** - bits of equipment, vitally important in the heat of the moment. Revolver ammo, bandages, drinking water, or the matches that light the way along a dark tunnel.

Supplies represent any equipment essential to a character's preparedness, the loss of which would render them vulnerable to physical harm or danger.

The player rolls an equipment's **Supplies Die** in the first pause after using that item – in combat this mostly means at the end of a fight, rather than every discharge of the gun. However, under extremes of stress, or say using guns like a submachine gun, the Player may roll after every Moment.

Sanity

Investigators constantly run into situations with horrible discoveries and bizarre monsters, and these threaten to overwhelm their sanity. When faced with horrific discoveries, the Investigator's limited grasp on sanity will be tested.

You can find more detail about losing and regaining **Sanity** from p 26 onward.

Investigation

Smokes and **Flashlights** are Investigative Resources. As an investigative game, these two Resources warrant detailed explanation.

If the Investigator needs to spot, uncover, research, stumble upon, recall, or otherwise physically discover something – that's a **Flashlight** roll.

If they might overhear, carouse, interrogate, coerce, fast talk, bribe, claim kinship or extract information through social connection or financial standing – that's a **Smokes** roll.

You break into an office at the docks and search the records. After searching for a few minutes, you find out that Pharaoh Shipping had an odd cargo arrive at a private quay and that it didn't go through normal customs checks or channels.

In this instance, you roll your Flashlight Die. If you get a 1 or 2, you drop the die size. You can still try to search for information, but when you drop to 1d4 and fail, you've run out of that resource. You can't search anymore.

Each use of **Flashlights** or **Smokes** provides a substantive, but self-contained, clue. The clue comes before the roll, so even a low roll will not leave the characters without options. Think of it in terms of a "Yes, and…" or a "Yes, but…" response to a character's line of questioning. Improvised theatre uses the "Yes, and …" response to provide a positive and open route to continue the scene, while a "Yes, but …" potentially stifles your opportunities. In this instance, you always get the "Yes" and the die result delivers the "and" or "but".

The difference is primarily dramatic, rather than a punishment – the player has already lost a dice step from a vital **Resource**! The GM can use the failed roll as an opportunity to spice up the narrative by throwing a potential spanner into the works. It hints at the spiraling loss of chances as Resources deplete.

Rolling any result except 1 or 2:

You find out that Pharaoh Shipping had an odd cargo and you note the manifest has been signed with a spidery scrawl – "L C Gilmore". Another reference to the Gilmore family. You gather up the papers and stow them. What do you do now?

Rolling a 1 or 2:

You find out that Pharaoh Shipping did indeed have an odd cargo delivered, the manifest signed off in cramped hand – "L C Gilmore". However, as you go to gather up the papers, you hear a creaking board and a beam of light slices across the window of the office. What do you do now?

What happens when you run out of Flashlights or Smokes? Does that mean you can't investigate any more? Yes, but not permanently.

If you run out of Flashlights, you're tired, vexed, unfocussed, burned out. You can't see the wood for the trees or you need to centre yourself to regain your loss of focus.

If you run out of Smokes, you ran your mouth off and brought the heat down. Or the locals have grown wary of the stranger with all those odd questions. You need to take a step back, leave town, or try another line of inquiry.

Investigative Recovery

Flashlights and Smokes recover at the end of an adventure. A generous GM can replenish them sooner during a multi-session investigation.

For example, the Investigator might recover a single step of Smokes by spending an evening in a seedy bar, playing cards in a gambling den or catching up with old contacts.

The Investigator who wants to replenish a Flashlight die could spend time in an academic institution's library in idle research, an evening cataloguing stamps, or make time for a period of mindful meditation.

Advantage & Disadvantage

A GM may decide that a course of action or task has a higher or lower chance of success.

For example, if the Investigator tries to save herself by doing something key to her **Occupation** or she attacks a sleeping target, Advantage could be appropriate.

In this instance, the player rolls an extra D20 to make the Save and the player chooses the preferred result. Generally, this is the result that benefits the player.

Conversely, if an Investigator places herself in danger by doing something utterly off-the-wall or she defends herself from an attack with an alarm clock, Disadvantage would certainly apply.

In this case, the GM will ask the player to roll an extra D20 and the GM chooses the preferred result. Most

Begin in media res; investigators in utterly alien, terrifying scenes.

often, this is the result that least benefits the player.

More rarely, the GM (or an Ability) may allow a Player to roll a Resource with Advantage. For example, an Investigator might take extra care using ammo during a fight by shooting only ever other Moment, or they might have an Ability that enhances library research.

Optional Rules

Throughout the core book you will find additional optional rules. They aren't essential to the game. More often that not, they offer a better chance of survival to the Investigators.

Discuss the addition of optional rules with the players, but remember that as the GM, you have the veto on the inclusion of any rule.

Assistance

An Investigator may choose to assist a colleague in a moment of peril. The support puts both in danger but enhances the chance of success. After the Gamemaster describes the Threat and the associated consequences, any player can offer to have their character assist, providing support seems reasonable.

The threatened Investigator faces the trouble and the assisted Player rolls with Advantage. The assisting Player rolls a Resource die. The descriptions under **Investigation** (see p 5) apply – for example, knowing or seeing something useful means a Flashlight roll.

If the assisted Player succeeds, then both Investigators manage to avoid the Threat. If the roll fails, with both dice rolling equal or higher to the Save value, both characters suffer. In addition, if the assisting Player rolls a 1 or 2, the Resource used drops a Die Step –the Gamemaster and Players can weave an appropriate story around the outcome.

Charles feels the sting as his flesh crisps, his feet pounding as he runs away from the strange ball of ethereal fire erupting from the study of the old mansion. Virginia, standing across the lobby, catches sight of the pursuing conflagration and cries strange words in an ancient tongue, intoning the words of an esoteric ward as a protection from elemental harm.

The GM agrees to allow the assist, meaning that Charles rolls two dice against his DEX of 12; if he rolls 12 or higher on both dice, the flames catch up with him and Virginia's moment of pause exposes her to the same danger. Regardless, Virginia's dabbling with the occult requires a test of her Sanity (see **Mythos Magic***, p 37).*

👾 <u>Fortune</u>

Investigators should be under no illusions – the odds are stacked high against them. The nature of the game should mean that Investigators fall (and fail) often, struck down by the inherent weakness of humanity versus the timeless persistence of the Mythos.

However, the GM can offer the Players <u>a pool of Fortune tokens – equal to</u> than <u>the number of Investigators plus one</u> – to ease their progress. These cover a whole investigation; anyone can <u>spend a Fortune to re-roll a failed</u> Save or Resource <u>check.</u>

If you use the optional **Adrenalin** rule (see p 29), a Fortune token cancels a forced roll.

The Campaign

The Cthulhu Hack is a game of horror. The game's mechanics seek to mirror the frailties and mortality of the 'heroes' in Lovecraft's stories. Investigators will face challenges like defeating mortal cults and revealing the nefarious plots of mad worshippers rather than unseating Azathoth from Its dark throne in the cacophonous heart of all Creation.

Investigator will die often in their ceaseless pursuit of the truth; success comes when they foil a plan, unseat a cackling mastermind or acquire possession of some artefact or tome. For the Gamemaster, a campaign of **The Cthulhu Hack** runs best if approached as a plan of action - the enemies plot laid out at every stage with their achievements outlined if left unchecked by outsiders.

The actions and interference of the Investigators will spoil that plan. They can extend the deadline of the planet's doom another day (though the beetles will inherit the Earth... it has been foretold in aeons past).

The Cthulhu Hack has a speedy process for character creation. A player should not fear the loss of a character - respawn comes quickly! Campaigns should best revolve around what lost investigators leave behind - journals, letters, wills, marginalia. The GM can scattered investigations over years, decades or even centuries, as the words of one group of foolhardy investigators falls into the hands of another.

An engaging campaign will arise from the cooperation of GM and players in creating a great story. Players should work hard to create strong and positive team bonds to give them something to rely on in an universe of cosmic uncertainty and indifference. By all means, everyone can have their dark little secrets, but the thrill of the game should come from achievements together; little personal victories can provide a cherry on the cake.

Inhabitants of a region, over whom the star Canopus rises nightly, live without sorrow.

Characters

Creating an Investigator

You define your Investigator in their ability to survive and their talent for eking the most out of their expertise, gear and connections.

The Cthulhu Hack measures these with **Saves** and **Resources** based on your choice of Archetype.

Saves cover the character's Physical potential – in **Strength**, **Dexterity**, **Constitution** – and the character's Personality – in their **Wisdom**, **Intelligence**, and **Charisma**.

Players generate each Save by rolling three 6-sided dice. Assign the scores to the Saves, in order; then, after rolling all six, the Player can swap two scores.

Alternatively, the GM can offer more control by allowing each player to roll all six scores and then assign the values to the Investigator's Saves. Whatever the method, if the Player rolls a Save with a value of 15 or more, they must roll the next value with only two 6-sided dice and add 2. After that, they can continue with three 6-sided dice, unless they roll another 15+.

The table is a guide to applying Saves in play and against what Threats.

Archetypes determine everything else about your character, with the player left to determine their personal story. Each Archetype (see the next section) sets values for Resources and lists some Special Abilities, with a selection of abilities to choose from.

The player should record all this detail on their personal character sheet.

STR	DEX	CON
Physical harm or hindrance you cannot dodge. Fighting hand to hand, holding a slathering beast at arm's length, or bench pressing a collapsing wall.	Physical harm or hindrance you can dodge. Dodging to avoid projectiles, sprinting through a crowd to catch a train, or taking a leap between rooftops.	Attempts to injure or impede with poison, disease, torture, or unavoidable harm - like an explosion. Knuckling down, staying awake or gritting teeth.

WIS	INT	CHA
Threat or hindrance through the distortion of the senses, deception, psychotropic drugs, or illusion; challenges requiring common sense or instinct.	Threat or hindrance through propapanda, magic, alien tech, or manipulation of scientific principles; challenges that demand a grasp of obscure lore or solving a fiendish puzzle.	Threat or hindrance using mind control, glamour, charm, or powers that wipe or overwhelm the personality; emotive or convincing words intent on delay or confusion.

View from window reveals a dark, dead world (or oddly changed) outside.

Quick Character Archetypes

To start quickly or if you're playing for the first time, choose an Archetype for your character. Each Archetype provides a standard build that sets out your character's:

- Investigative Resources and Sanity
- Hit Dice and Hit Points
- Special Abilities, which can simplify or enhance rolls to Save or check Resources, and
- Starting Wealth

The Player can choose an Archetype that appeals to them or the GM might provide guidance. Each Archetype favours one or more Saves, and a player would be wise to choose an Archetype that fits their Save values.

Archetype and play style are linked to some extent. If you want to play games with a strong investigative angle, like Lovecraft's own stories, you might want to stick with Scholars and Philanthropists.

If you plan on playing adventures with a pulpier theme, with set piece fights and a selection of physical and cerebral activities, a mix of Archetypes will work best with Adventurers as the default selection.

The GM should guide the focus for Archetypes based on the sort of Investigations they have planned.

After selecting an Archetype, choose an occupation and two pieces of starting gear.

Occupation: If your Investigator faces a Save where the expertise of their occupation might assist, roll with Advantage.

Gear: Discuss starting gear with your GM. Choose unique and personal items that exemplify your occupation, motivations, beliefs and history.

Archetype Notes

Saves: Each Archetype lists a Prime Save and two Other Saves. Listed Saves are like a recommendation for the type; you're free to ignore it. The **Prime Save** has the additional benefit that when checking for Experience (p14), roll with Advantage.

Special Abilities: Archetypes have a fixed Special Ability. The player then selects two more Abilities from the three listed. Investigators that survive an adventure can expand their Special Abilities (see **Experience**).

Inhabitants of an ancient estate do all things to ancient ceremony; nothing new is found.

Adventurer

Sleuth, Explorer, Archaeologist, Private Eye, Soldier of Fortune

Flashlights/Smokes: D8/D6
Hit Dice: D8 / Starting HP: 1d8 + 8
Wealth: CHA x 3 (WD: D8)
Sanity Die: D8
Damage 1d6 Armed / 1d4 Unarmed
Prime Saves: DEX; Others: CON, STR

Special Abilities

Swings & Leaps. Roll with Advantage on Saves when performing athletic tasks, like: climbing, jumping, leaping, swinging, flipping.

Choose <u>two</u> from the following:

Scrounger. You can offset the loss of an item of equipment's Resource Die by losing an Investigation Die instead.
Slippery Customer. Once per session your slippery nature allows you to shift the repercussions of a failed INT or WIS Save to someone else.
Steady Hand. Once per game hour, you automatically succeed with a single Ranged Armed Attack.

Philanthropist

Alienist, Doctor, Dilettante, Clergyman, Dot Com Frontman

Flashlights/Smokes: D6/D10
Hit Die: D8 / Starting HP: 1d8 + 8
Wealth: CHA x 4 (WD: D10)
Sanity Die: D10
Damage: 1d6 Armed / 1 Unarmed
Prime Save: WIS; Others: CHA, CON

Special Abilities

Indomitable. Roll with Advantage when making a Save against deception, mind control or attempts to cloud perception.

Choose <u>two</u> from the following:

Field Medicine. Once per gaming hour, outside combat, a Philanthropist can heal another character 1d6 lost Hit Points (or one Hit Die Step, if using the optional rules).
Grim Determination. Once per gaming session, you can re-roll any check for Out of the Action or Sanity/Shock – choose the preferred result.
Withering Words. You can use CHA for attacks (instead of STR or DEX), providing your opponent can hear and understand you. Roll damage as if Armed; if reduced to 0hp (or no Hit

Ruffian

Charlatan, Criminal, Enforcer, Bondsman, Smuggler, Gun Runner

Flashlights/Smokes: D6/D10
Hit Die: D6 / Starting HP: 1d6 + 8
Wealth: Special
Sanity Die: D8
Damage: 1d6 Armed / 1d4 Unarmed
Prime Save: CHA; Others: WIS, DEX

Special Abilities

Self-Preservation. Roll with Advantage when making a Save to avoid traps, devices or other mechanisms intended to impede or harm.

Choose two from the following:

Better Alone. While fighting without an ally, you temporarily gain 2 Armour Points and inflict +2 Armed damage with melee weapons.

House of Cards. Once per game session, you can break a trust or betray an ally or friend – and narrate what happens – to avoid damage from a failed WIS or CHA Save.

Sizing Up. You have a keen eye for weakness; gain +1 to Hit and Damage an opponent at a cost of making a Flashlight roll after every such attack.

Scholar

Professor, Archivist, Clerk, Nurse, Academic, Tabletop Game Designer

Flashlights/Smokes: D8/D12, D10/D10 or D12/D8
Hit Die: D4 / Starting HP: 1d4 + 8
Wealth: CHA x 2   (WD: D6)
Sanity Die: D8
Damage: 1d4 Armed / 1 Unarmed
Prime Save: INT; Others: CHA, WIS

Special Abilities

Deduction. Once per game session, you can apply your powers of deduction and reasoning to reach an apposite conclusion; the GM must provide a hint to the next best step.

Choose two from the following:

Iron Mind. Roll with Advantage on Saves when resisting magic, occult ritual, hexes, curses, or possession by alien influences.

Erudite. Once per game hour, you can automatically succeed with a single INT or WIS Save.

MacGyver. Once per session, you can improvise a solution to a situation using available tools, devices, and uncommon lore.

Freeform Characters

Creating characters using one of the Archetypes makes it quick to start. However, if you plan an ongoing series of adventures, Players may appreciate the option to create unique characters. This section provides a system to support modular character creation. Aside from a few basic dice rolls for Saves, much of the process allows the Player to decide the shape and expertise of their Investigator.

Saves

Roll six times, using the standard dice mechanic. Once rolled, the player can assign the scores to their Saves as desired. Assign one Save as your **Prime Save**. When you survive an adventure, you can roll for improvement in this **Save with Advantage**.

Dice

Share 14 steps of dice across all base abilities: **Hit Die**, **Sanity**, **Flashlights**, **Smokes**, **Armed**, and **Unarmed**. You must spend at least one Die on each, with the exception of Unarmed. If you place no dice in **Unarmed**, you only ever inflict a single point of damage on a successful unarmed attack. Roll Investigator **Hit Points** as **Hit Die + 8**.

Special Abilities

You start with three **Special Abilities** selected from the following list. You gain an additional Special Ability when you survive an investigation (see **Experience**).

- **Adrenalin Rush.** Once per game hour, while in combat, recover a Hit Die of lost HP (or one **Hit Die Step**, see p 18).
- **Animal Handler.** You roll with Advantage when handling, riding or challenged by common animals.
- **Backfire.** Once per game hour, you can automatically succeed in a defensive Save and cause the attacker to damage themselves, suffering the damage of their own weapon.
- **Better Alone.** While fighting without an ally, you temporarily gain 2 Armour Points and inflict +2 Armed damage with melee weapons.
- **Deadeye.** Increase ranged damage by one step (if currently 1, raise to 1d4).
- **Improved Deadeye.** Requires Deadeye; check for Upper Hand (see p 25) or spin about and fall prone.
- **Deduction.** Once per game session, you can apply your powers of deduction and reasoning to reach

Two souls appear to have murdered each other; found locked within an improbable room.

an apposite conclusion - and require the GM to provide a hint to the next best step.

- **Erudite.** Once per gaming hour, you can automatically succeed with a single INT or WIS Save.
- **Field Medicine.** Once per gaming hour, outside combat, you can heal another character 1d6 lost Hit Points (or one Hit Die Step, if using the optional rules).
- **Grim Determination.** Once per gaming session, you can re-roll any check for Out of the Action or Sanity / Shock - choose your preferred result.
- **Hardy.** You roll with Advantage when making Saves to avoid the harmful effects of poison, drugs, chemicals, or alcohol.
- **Heavy Hitter.** Increase melee damage by one step (if currently 1, raise to D4).
- **Improved Heavy Hitter.** Requires Heavy Hitter; DEX Save to disarm your opponent on a successful strike.
- **House of Cards.** Once per game session, you can break a trust or betray an ally or friend – and narrate what happens – to avoid damage from a failed WIS or CHA Save.
- **Indomitable.** Roll with Advantage when making a Save against deception, mind control or attempts to cloud perception.
- **Influential.** Gain an additional step in Smokes. You can select this Ability multiple times.

- **Inheritance.** Gain an additional step in **Wealth** (**Wealth as Resource**, see p 20). You can select this Ability multiple times. You can automatically succeed a Wealth roll once per investigation.
- **Iron Mind.** Roll with Advantage on Saves when resisting magic, occult ritual, hexes, curses, or possession by alien influences.
- **Jack in the Hole.** Once per game session, you can sidestep a failed CHA or WIS Save by leveraging your network of friends, associates and unspent favours.
- **Legerdemain.** You roll with Advantage with tasks of hand-eye coordination, like sleight of hand, picking pockets, and manipulating small and fragile tools and objects.
- **Like a Rock.** While standing still you temporarily gain 2 Armour Points and do +2 melee damage, but make DEX Saves at -2.
- **Lockpicker.** You can crack any lock by making a Flashlight roll.
- **Improved Lockpicker** – Requires Lockpicker; but, you can roll with Advantage.
- **MacGyver.** Once per session, you can improvise a solution to a situation using available tools, devices, and uncommon lore.
- **Mechanic.** You roll with Advantage when repairing or damaging machinery or vehicles.
- **Narrow Escape.** Once per game session, you can break a piece of equipment – and narrate what

happens - to avoid damage from a failed STR or DEX Save.

- **Pugilist.** Increase unarmed damage by one step (if currently 1, raise to D4).
- **Improved Pugilist.** Requires Pugilist; instead of inflicting extra damage, roll 1d6 – if 1 or 2, cripple one of your opponent's limbs.
- **Ripped.** You roll with Advantage when making a Save to lift, drag, snap, break, wrestle or otherwise exert your strength.
- **Robust.** You benefit from natural protection in Melee combat, reducing weapon damage against you by one step. You can select this Ability multiple times.
- **Savvy.** You gain an additional step in Flashlights. You can select this Ability multiple times.
- **Scrounger.** You can offset the loss of an item of equipment's Resource Die by losing an investigation die instead.
- **Improved Scrounger.** Requires Scrounger; plus, always roll Ammo die with Advantage.
- **Self-Preservation.** Roll with Advantage when making a Save to avoid traps, devices and other mechanisms intended to impede or harm.
- **Sizing Up.** You have a keen eye for weakness; gain a +1 to Hit and Damage at a cost of rolling Flashlights after every such attack.
- **Slippery Customer.** Once per session your slippery nature allows you to shift the repercussions of a failed INT or WIS Save to someone else.
- **Stagecraft.** You roll with Advantage when entertaining, performing or making Reaction rolls to avoid harm or consequence.
- **Steady Hand.** Once per game hour, you can auto-succeed with a single Ranged attack.
- **Improved Steady Hand.** Requires Steady Hand; you do not have to roll DEX Saves to hit (unless at Disadvantage) with any Ranged weapon but must roll a Supply Die immediately.
- **Surprise Attack.** In the first moment of any combat, you can inflict twice the normal damage with the weapon in hand.
- **Swings & Leaps.** Roll with Advantage on Saves when performing athletic tasks, like climbing, jumping, leaping, swinging, flipping.
- **Tactical Advantage.** As part of your action, you can make an additional attack against the same or a different target. You can select this Ability multiple times.
- **Withering Words.** You can use CHA for attacks (instead of STR or DEX), providing your opponent can hear and understand you. Roll damage as if Armed; if you reduce an opponent to 0 hp (or no Hit Dice), they become incapacitated.

Soul seeks cause for partners disappearance; nightly descends into earth of the graveyard.

Experience

At the end of each adventure, an Investigator gains a measure of expertise. Players should keep a record of how many investigations their character survive.

Between adventures, as well as recovering from all damage and having the chance to recover sanity (see **Insanity**, p 26), Players should:

Roll their Hit Dice – the player can either take this result as their character's new Hit Points or keep the old number. If they had the highest value for the dice and roll that number, step up to the next higher Hit Dice.

Choose a Save and roll 1d20 – if the result is higher than the current score for that Save, increase the value by 1.

Choose a new Special Ability – select a new ability from the list.

Hit Points and Hit Dice

Hit Points signpost the harm you can withstand before sustaining a life-threatening injury. Archetypes state the **Hit Die** used for rolling Hit Points, modified during character generation by adding 8 to the result. Freeform characters always start with **1d8 + 8**.

Out of Action

A character with zero (or fewer) Hit Points is taken Out of Action (OofA). They fall prone or stagger about, struck almost dumb with pain. Out of danger (usually at the end of combat), roll 1d10 on the table. If they survive, they regain 1d4 HP (up to maximum).

OUT OF ACTION (roll 1d10, unless told otherwise)

1	**Dead** - Not alive anymore.
2	**Broken** - Deduct 6 points from Save scores permanently, choosing at least two scores to reduce or spreading the loss across several.
3	**Savaged** – Deduct 4 points from Personality Save scores permanently, choosing either one to reduce or spreading the loss across more than one.
4	**Crippled** – Deduct 2 points from Physical Save scores permanently, choosing either one to reduce or spreading the loss across more than one.
5	**Cracked Bones** – All Physical Save scores reduced by -4 until the end of the next day or the end of this gaming session, whichever comes first.
6	**Knocked out** - Knocked out until the end of the current Scene.
7	**Mild Concussion** – Disadvantage on all Tests for the next 20 minutes.
8	**Staggered** – Disadvantage on all Tests for the next 10 minutes.
9+	**Winded** – Disadvantage on all Tests for the next minute.

Strange and immortal animal who speaks in a language horrifying and revelatory.

Hit Dice As Resource

Instead of a fixed score, you can handle damage with the Hit Die itself, like any other Resource Die. This approach means less book-keeping and slightly more resilient characters.

When hurt, a Player rolls their **Hit Dice Resource** (HDR), with a 1 or 2 stepping down. **Out of Action** kicks in when the 1d4 steps down. Aside from **Field Medicine**, hospitalisation restores Hit Dice at a rate of 1 HD per day, while light activity and rest restores just 1 HD every third day. For **Armour and Cover**, see p21.

Big Damage Hurts

Hit Dice Resource (HDR) works with opponents of similar power, but when you start using big guns or monsters it makes less sense. If battling a Shoggoth, something's got to give as that Crush attack is no small beans.

When an Investigator takes a hit, check the **column** with their **current Hit Die** on the table, then read across to find the damage inflicted within the ranges shown. The Player then rolls their Hit Die with the penalty (or benefit) indicated.

Powerful attacks may mean having to make rolls with **Disadvantage** or **Double Disadvantage** – roll three dice and take the worst. Weak attacks mean the opposite against someone with robust Hit Dice, allowing them to roll with **Advantage** or even **Double Advantage** - roll three dice and take the best.

Armour and **cover** (AP) adjust the amount of damage (see p 24) <u>before</u> reading across the chart.

A robust Investigator (HD 12) faces off against a Shoggoth and suffers the full weight of the gelatinous entities Crush (damage 18). Without any armour or cover to cushion the blow, reading across the HD 12 row shows that any damage of 12+ means rolling Hit Dice Resource at Double Disadvantage. However, in this instance, the Investigator has managed to dive behind a section of ruined wall laced with weird iridescent alien metals (offering AP 9),

HD	Double Advantage	Advantage	Normal Roll	Disadvantage	Double Disadvantage
4	n/a	1	2	3	4+
6	n/a	1	2-3	4-5	6+
8	n/a	1-2	3-4	5-7	8+
10	1	2-3	4-6	7-9	10+
12+	1-2	3-4	5-7	8-11	12+

BIG DAMAGE, BIG DISADVANTAGE — *WHAT USERS ROLL WITH →* (handwritten)

USERS HD VS DAMAGE INFLICTED BY OPPONENT → (handwritten)

Blackened pictures; subjects undecipherable. Restoration = Revelation. (handwritten)

reducing the attack to 9 damage, which means the player merely suffers Disadvantage on the HDR check

Rolled Damage

If you have an outbreak of **Player vs Player**, which means rolled damage values instead of stating a fixed result (as per normal combat), or you like to roll for harm when an antagonist strikes a successful blow, either:

Roll the Damage: Roll as normal and compare the outcome of the roll against the ranges in the table.

For example, a cultist armed with a pistol shoots a HD 6 Ruffian at point blank range. If the GM rolls a 6 on 1d6 for the pistol the poor Investigator must roll her HDR with Double Disadvantage.

Half the Die Type: Take the size of the Die and half it. A D6 attack does 3; a D10 attack does 5. If you're rolling multiple dice for some reason, add all the Die sizes together and then add half the number of dice rolled.

For example, the player has found some hideous Mi-Go blasting gun that does 4d4 damage. If the GM chooses to use the fixed damage method, it inflicts ((4+4+4+4)/2) + 2 (half the number of dice) = 10 damage with every strike. Against any opponent, up to HD 10, it will force a HDR check with Double Disadvantage.

Wealth and Equipment

All Investigators start with cash in their pocket – based on a multiple of their **CHA Save** indicated by the archetype.

Freeform Investigators – and Ruffians – roll **1d6** on the **Starting Wealth** table to determine their initial funds. The first column generates standard cash, the second a Wealth Die value (see **Wealth as Resource**, p 20).

STARTING WEALTH (roll 1d6)		
1	CHAx1	D4
2-3	CHAx2	D6
4-5	CHAx3	D8
6	CHAx4	D10 and owes a debt

Currency

The starting cash assumes US dollars and that you set the game in the 1920/1930s, the time associated with Lovecraft's own stories. If you're running a modern game, multiply all starting cash values by fifty.

If a character needs a piece of equipment, look for a modern equivalent. If you're running a 1920s game, divide the cost of an item by 50. That isn't precise, but it'll be close.

You can find a fair number of resources online that list estimates for the relative value of currency in any given year. On the other hand, this is a game, so play it by ear.

For example, running a modern game in the UK, an Adventurer with CHA 10 starts with £1,500. Keepsakes aside, the player wants a shotgun. A check online finds that picking up a brand new one will set them back around £1,000, or they can pick up one for half that on the secondary market.

Wealth as Resource

You can choose to abstract wealth and add a new Resource. Using this approach, an Investigator starts with a Wealth Die based on their Archetype (see the value in brackets).

When the Investigator makes a purchase, that's more than pocket change, roll the Wealth Die.

A 1 or 2 means they make the purchase, but they've depleted their reserves. Losing the final D4 means they're out of cash and overstepped their credit.

At the end of any adventure where a character depleted their Wealth to zero, have them make a roll with their undepleted base Wealth Die. On a 1 or 2, their Wealth Die drops a step.

A character can increase their Wealth Die at the end of an adventure by selecting a suitable Ability for their Experience.

The Bruiser

The first edition of **The Cthulhu Hack** included the combative Bruiser, an archetype that didn't easily fit the themes set out in Lovecraft's stories but that worked from a roleplaying point of view.

For those who want more fisticuffs than fact-finding, the archetype is:

Bruiser

Flashlights/Smokes: D4/D4
Hit Die: D10 / Starting HP: 1d10 + 8
Wealth: Special (as Ruffian)
Sanity Die: D8
Damage: 1d8 Armed / 1d6 Unarmed
Prime Save: STR; Others: DEX, CON

Special Abilities

Tactical Advantage. You can make an additional attack against the same or a different target.

Choose <u>two</u> from the following:

Ripped. Roll with Advantage when making a Save to lift, drag, snap, break, wrestle or exert your strength.
Narrow Escape. Once per game session, you can break a piece of equipment – and narrate what happens - to avoid damage from a failed STR or DEX Save.
Adrenalin Rush. Once per game hour, while in combat, recover a Hit Die of lost HP.

Secret language, all but forgotten, spoken by elders in wild country, leads to hidden marvels.

Threats

The Player's Turn

When faced with some form of determined or prolonged Threat, the speed of the game changes. While fisticuffs and firefights don't strictly represent Lovecraft's fiction, gamers sometimes find a brawl or a firefight helps to break up the more intense scenes of an investigation with something more pulp.

When conflict erupts, you will start to deal with time in a more abstract way.

Time

There are three important types of tracked in-game time – Moments, Minutes and Scenes.

Moments are used during combat and fast paced scenes of danger. They represent a quick flurry of activity – something that might happen in a few seconds. You might fire a few shots wildly, duck for cover, or yell instructions to a colleague.

Minutes are used when exploring or investigating. They usually apply when you're concerned about duration – like how long it will take to travel across town to the library or when you'll regain consciousness after a blow to the back of the head.

Scenes cover the period it takes for the Investigators to resolve a challenge, best an opponent, or handle a situation at a specific location. The GM can keep the definition intentionally loose but should indicate when a Scene ends and a new one begins.

A further sort of time exists, but it relates to the real world. Some Abilities and Spells, for example, refer to Game Hours or Sessions. It means you should keep an eye on the clock to see when you can next use an ability or when something wears off. A Session refers to the period you spend gaming on a single day or before taking a long break.

Movement and Distance

Rather than track precise distance, The Cthulhu Hack uses abstract range: Close, Nearby, Far Away and Distant. In a Moment, a character can move somewhere Nearby as well as

CLOSE (C)	NEARBY (N)	FAR AWAY (F)	DISTANT (D)
Up to 5 feet	5 -59 feet	60 - 119 feet	120 feet or more

Monstrous accident leaves hollow, haunted derelict; invisible thing felt or glimpsed in wreck

complete another action, like an attack. A character can forgo their action and move somewhere Far Away – which takes a whole Moment. Anything beyond that is Distant – reached in two whole Moments.

For converting existing movement rates or measures (from other games or adventures) use the range table as a rough guide; keep in mind that this is not a tactical game!

Fighting

When a character attacks they roll a STR Save for Melee or a DEX Save for a Ranged attack.

The simplified flow of the game means that when an Investigator makes a Save, they both attempt to inflict harm and avoid getting hurt themselves. Attacking is a basic action (see **Initiative and Actions**, below).

The GM might call for other Saves – like a WIS Save might resist an attack on the mind.

Range: To make a Melee Attack an opponent must be Close. On the other hand, Ranged Attacks against Close opponents are possible but rolled for with Disadvantage.

Antagonists: Enemies deal damage based on their Hit Die and any **Special Abilities**, and they cause damage

when player characters fail their attack rolls. If total attacks a creature, or group of creatures, can inflict exceeds the number of characters attacks, the players must Save to defend (Multiple Attacks, p 31).

Powerful opponents make hard targets, because of their resilience and their ability to overpower. Armour affects the damage an opponent suffers; To-Hit (T-H) modifies the Save target, making attacks harder.

AVERAGE ANTAGONIST			
HD	DMG	ARMOUR	T-H
1	2/1d4	n/a	n/a
2	3/1d6	1	-1
3	4/1d8	2	-2
4	5/1d10	3	-3
5	6/1d12	4	-4
6	7/2d6	5	-5
7	8/1d6+1d8	6	-6
8	9/2d8	7	-7
9	10/1d8+1d10	8	-8
10	11/2d10	9	-9
11	12/1d10+1d12	10	-10
12	13/2d12	10	-11

Initiative and Actions

Whether fighting an opponent or struggling against some puzzle-trap, they're all just Threats; everyone has the chance to save themselves. Let the players act in any order they choose.

Sounds - possibly musical - heard in the night from other worlds or realms of being.

Each character can take a basic action, move a short distance and say a few words. Anything that sounds or feels complicated takes longer.

Common foes tend to act after the Investigators. Mythos foes or notable enemies act simultaneously (see **Mythos Foes**, p 31).

If an action takes longer, make a note or set a dice in front of the player showing the number of actions that remain to complete the long task. Whenever they act, they can continue their efforts, and reduce the number on the die, or do something else.

The investigators find themselves trapped between a warehouse and a gang of mobsters in cover behind some crates. They could make their escape if only they could start their car, but it won't start.

The GM states that any character can attempt to fix it, but it will take three Moments of effort. A die set down on the table shows "3", as a reminder. Each time a character has a chance to act, they can do their own thing or focus on getting the car started.

Sometimes, the GM might choose to use a similar mechanic to note the passage of time before something bad happens – referred to as a **Countdown**. In this case, the GM will state the number of Moments and whether the Investigators can do something to avoid it, then set the die.

Damage

Attacks deal damage based on fighting aptitude. If you have a high-value attack die, you're capable regardless of the weapon used.

The **Armed Die** is damage inflicted with a proper weapon, whether ranged or melee.

The **Unarmed Die** is fighting bare knuckled or using something improvised, like a chair leg or tire iron.

Roll the die and deduct it from the opponent's Hit Points, accounting for Armour and Cover.

If the player fails their Save versus a threat, it hurts them or they suffer a setback. The GM can choose to strike off one of an Antagonist's attacks or they can narrate how the situation works against the Investigator (though it shouldn't hurt them, as the GM chose not to commit an attack to generate harm).

Antagonists inflict damage based on their Hit Die and Special Abilities. The table on p23 shows default damage – a number followed by one or more dice. The GM can choose to either inflict a fixed default or roll. **Creatures of the Mythos** (see p 34) assumes the default.

Creatures of the Mythos do the damage listed, or the default from the table if nothing is listed. The GM can create opponents on the fly by setting their Hit Die and using the information on the **Average Antagonist** table; like a Cultist (HD 2) or a Hellhound (HD 4).

🐙 Upper Hand

Some Abilities generate secondary effects. To test if an Investigator can get the Upper Hand, <u>roll the same dice as the Antagonist's damage dice</u> (as outlined in the **Average Antagonist** table, p 23). <u>On a 1 or 2, the Upper Hand effect applies.</u> Otherwise, normal damage applies.

Lord August fires on a Deep One using Improved Deadeye. As well as improved damage, if he gains the Upper Hand the target spins and falls prone. As the Deep One has HD 2, the player rolls a 1d6 to determine the outcome; but even without a 1 or 2, he will inflict the extra damage of Deadeye.

🐙 (Im)Perfect Results

If a player rolls an attack with a perfect 1 (without modification), they **inflict double** the result of the damage dice they roll.

If a player rolls a perfect 20 (without modification), they **suffer double damage**, with cover or armour applying as normal.

SPECIAL WEAPONS			
TYPE	SUPPLY DIE	RNG	+DMG Step / -ToHit / Notes
Revolver	D6	N	Concealable
Pistol	D8	N	None
Hunting Rifle	D6	F	Rng: D w/ tripod. 1D10 Armed Dmg.
Shotgun	D6	N	+2 step / -2 to hit. Target Armour counts double.
Machinegun	D8	N	Shot or Spray: auto-hit, immediate SD
Sniper Rifle	D6	D	Miss an action to auto-hit next action. 1d12 Armed Dmg.
Grenade	n/a	3x STR	+3 step / -3 to hit, effects 1d4 targets in a Nearby area
Pepper Spray	D6	N	Avoid attacks (defend) with Advantage for 1d3 Moments; Concealable
BFG	D8	F	Roll 1D12 Armed Dmg with Advantage, roll Supply Die with Disadvantage

Vague lights or visions seen of other world or place when eyes closed; connected, terrible.

Special Weapons

<u>Special weapons have features that change the way combat works.</u> You may have to roll your **Supply Die** more often, miss an action to aim, or prepare additional equipment, like a tripod, to achieve the maximum effect.

For example, an Investigator with an Armed Die 1d4 uses a Shotgun against a ghoul at Close range. The Shotgun, at that distance, raises a characters Armed Die to 1d8 (+2 steps) but suffers a -2 modifier on their Save.

Armour and Cover

Armour: Access to armour depends on the setting and the GMs approval.

Antagonists generally do have armour. The Creatures of the Mythos section lists Armour Points (AP), as appropriate. If you create your own Antagonists, use the value on the Average Antagonist table. APs max out at 10.

<u>Armour reduces damage. To calculate damage inflicted, roll and then deduct the AP value.</u>

The Investigator from the example in the last section shot the Ghoul with a Shotgun. The Ghoul has 3 Hit Dice and no specific reference to Armour, so the GM assumes Armour 2. The

Investigator rolls a 6, so the Ghoul loses 4 hit points (6 – 2).

Cover: <u>Cover provides protection like Armour and an extra pool of Hit Points.</u> In addition, <u>a character has Advantage on their Save to defend if at least half covered at greater than Close range</u> – so, crouched behind a car or a low wall, for example, while taking pot-shots.

ARMOUR	
Leather, padding clothing	1 AP (+0 HP)
Reinforced	2 AP (+0 HP)
Layered weave, plated	3 AP (+5 HP)*

COVER	
Wood	1 AP (5 HP)
Brick	3 AP (15 HP)
Reinforced Glass	5 AP (25 HP)
Metal	9 AP (45 HP)

* Heavier armour can also offer an expanded pool of Hit Points that depletes like normal HP. Roll a d6 Resource Die after combat. 3-6, recover the HP; 1-2, the armour requires repair. Repairs will take time and probably Wealth.

Insanity

Sanity is a character's hold on reality and their senses. When confronted by situations likely to dehumanise or loosen the character's sense of the real, roll the die. <u>If the roll is 1-2 then the Sanity Die is downgraded to the next lower die in the standard chain</u>

(see Resources, p 3). Make a Sanity test when:

- Stranger attacks without reason, with intent to kill
- Friend or family member attacks you without reason, with intent to kill
- Suffer traumatic personal injury
- Witness the death of a stranger
- Witness the death of a friend or family
- Witness an event that defies explanation
- Encounter a supernatural or alien being or a sentient mechanical construct
- Discover a dismembered body or horrifically mutilated survivor
- Witness a particularly gruesome or bestial assault

When the Sanity Die downgrades, the character experiences a moment of temporary insanity. Roll 1d6, on the table below. The effect persists as indicated or for the rest of the Scene. Sanity can never be higher than the die you start.

When you roll a 1-2 on a D4 Sanity Die the character goes permanently insane. Say farewell to your character. With the agreement of the

TEMPORARY INSANITY (roll 1d6)

1 **Amnesia** - The Investigator forgets a significant event, location or individual, possibly unconnected with the source of madness - or simply connected in a tangential or subliminal way. All references to the thing draws a blank or triggers an emotive outburst.

2 **Blackout** - The Investigator passes out. They lose all awareness of anything that happens during this blackout. Under stress (any potential loss of Sanity) for the next Scene, the character must make a **CON Save** or blackout again.

3 **Paranoia** – The Investigator trusts nothing and no one. Everything has an agenda at odds with their wellbeing. The smallest action or word holds hidden meaning - trust no one and stay sharp for treachery.

4 **Hysteria** – The Investigator devolves into a tumult of screaming hysterics, unable to acknowledge whatever triggered their state. The Investigator takes 2 hit points damage; anyone in **Close** range must make a **DEX Save** to avoid 1 damage. Hysteria persists for a Minute.

5 **Paralysis** – The character freezes, gripped by fear. They cannot move of their own accord for a **Minute**. Other characters can attempt to carry them or drag them, but they're deadweight until they recover - which requires a successful CON Save. Failing leaves them statue-like and imperiled.

6 **Delusions** - The Investigator cannot make sense of the world nor rely on what they know. They question everything and likely believes things others cannot see, understand or agree upon.

Prehistoric inhabitants preserved perfectly frozen in Siberian ice.

GM, you may complete a final emotive scene, but that scene should not serve as a Deus ex Machina intervention into a difficult plot line or situation. No derailing the plot in your last moments when you've allowed your character to nose-dive into insanity.

The Weight of Horror

The basic Sanity rules assume that all scares scare alike; all horrors, however, are not equal.

The GM should judge the sense of connection or cosmic wrongness before having the Player make a Sanity roll and adjust accordingly:

- Impersonal Horror - Make Sanity roll at Advantage.
- Personal Horror - Make a standard Sanity roll.
- Incomprehensible Horror - Make Sanity roll at Disadvantage

Shock

The Sanity rules hit Investigators hard and affect them significantly. The disorientating alien assault of the very existence of the Mythos should challenge sanity at every turn.

However, the danger of insanity might seem too extreme. In this case, consider Shock.

When a Sanity test shows a 1 or 2, use the Shock instead of Temporary Insanity table.

Most of the results last for only Moments. When Shocked, Players can use tokens to track the effect; when their turn comes, they return a token and continue to suffer.

When the last token goes, the Investigator recovers.

SHOCK (roll 1d6)

1 **Shaking** -1d6 modifier on **DEX Saves** for the same number of Moments. Penalty reduces -1 each Moment that passes.

2 **Vague** - Mental **Disadvantage (Save)** for the next 1d6 Moments.

3 **Rabbit** – No Physical actions or Saves are possible for the next Moment. Stands motionless.

4 **Faint** – Takes another character a Moment to revive. **STR/DEX/INT** are at **Disadvantage** for an additional 1d3 Moments.

5 **Dive** – No action possible, other than to hide for the next 1d3 Moments.

6 **Scream** - Piercing scream. Attracts attention.

As dinosaurs were once surpassed by mammals, so will man be surpassed by insect or bird.

🐙 Adrenalin

Protagonists often ride the surge of their fear. They know that the horror might end them, so they keep pushing on, at a price. You can do the same in The Cthulhu Hack.

Investigators start with two Adrenalin tokens. Use a token with two clearly different sides – like a coin or pieces from a Reversi game – establishing a consistent side as spent.

An investigator faced with a Sanity test can choose to push on. Spend the token and turn it over. The Sanity test auto-succeeds AND the Investigator gets a +1 for each Adrenalin coin *spent* before, applied to their next Save. They can only spend one token at a time; when they spend the second, they get a +2 on their next Save.

Using Adrenalin is not without cost. The GM can, at any time, return a point of Adrenalin to a player and use it to reveal a Horrible Truth.

The GM chooses one of the following:

- Force the re-roll of a Save just rolled
- Force a Resource test for a piece of gear or weapon
- Add a previously undeclared Threat to the current Scene
- Place an innocent in immediate danger

- Force a Player to immediately throw for **Shock** (p 28), without loss of a Sanity step
- Force the Player to detail a dark revelation about their character

Once returned, the Adrenalin becomes available for the player to use again.

Healing

Investigators recover health through rest and recuperation. They never gain more than their maximum rolled Hit Points nor do they ever go below zero.

Immediate Recovery: If a character rendered Out of Action receives medical attention and presses to re-join combat, deduct the number they rolled on the OofA table from 8; they spend that many Moments recovering before they get back on their feet. Surviving a OofA roll leaves them with only 1d4 HP, so they had best find something sturdy to hide behind.

Daily: For each day with adequate rest, characters recover a Hit Die of Hit Points (or a Die Step of Hit Dice, if using the optional rules) and a single Die Step of Investigative Resource - Smokes or Flashlights, player's choice.

Long Term: Sanity recovers more slowly. A character that did not lose all their Sanity can recover a Die Step after a full week of rest, with 1d4 weeks per Die Step thereafter.

Daemons seeking human form for evil purpose take on the bodies of the condemned.

A character reduced to D4 would rise to D6 after a week, and D8 after up to a month. The GM could allow a character to engage in restorative activities to regain an extra die.

Incarceration: A character that loses all their Sanity (lose the last D4) requires sanatorium treatment. The player and GM need to discuss whether to have the character return at a later date or just roll a new one.

Antagonists

Antagonist Hit Die

Hit Dice represent an opponent's power and potential to both cause and sustain harm. The GM determines an Antagonist's Hit Points by rolling an number of d8s equal to their Hit Dice.

When generating more than one opponent a GM can use the same value for similar entities. For a quick calculation, assume Hit Points equal the number of Hit Dice x 4.

Powerful Opponents

For every Hit Die an opponent has above the first, modify the Save of an Investigator fighting it by -1 (this is called the **To-Hit modifier**)

An Investigator with STR 10 fighting against a monster with HD 5 would make their Save against a modified target of 6 (10-4).

Reaction

In most investigations the Antagonists will possess predetermined attitudes and goals that guide the GM in choosing their likely actions.

Under circumstances where the adventure has no notes about attitude or you create an encounter on the fly, you can roll 1d8 on the Reaction Table to determine a random attitude or motivation (or choose one):

D8	REACTION
1	**Flee**: shy, scared, scouting
2	**Avoid**: guilty, demoralised
3	**Testing**: wary, questioning
4	**Quid Pro Quo**: trade, gossip
5	**Convert**: subvert, persuade
6	**Mischief**: mislead, ill will
7	**Rob**: deprive, subdue, hinder
8	**Hate**: kill, destroy, sacrifice

Common Foes

You can create most common people and creatures based on information from the **Average Antagonist** table (see p 23).

To add variety, you can give them more than one attack, splitting the damage. The split doesn't need to be precise – so, a Grizzly Bear, as a HD 4, might have two Claw (3) attacks, rather than a single attack that inflicts 5 damage.

You can also adapt ideas from the Creatures of the Mythos section (p 34). The Grizzly Bear might cause a Bite (3) if both Claws hit the same opponent, similar to the way a Byakhee attacks.

Mythos Foes

Creatures of the Mythos are not in any way ordinary. Most have multiple attacks, access to Mythos Magic, use of strange technology and other odd aspects intended to emphasize the otherworldliness of their existence.

As a general rule, use the Average Antagonist table, but increase the Damage inflicted by 50 - 100%. In some cases, this will come as a single attack (like the Shoggoth's crush) or many.

Battling any creature of the Mythos should not be fair. The darkness will prevail and investigators will fall. Best to balance prudence with daring, and know when to run away.

Multiple Attacks

Where a creature (or an ordinary human antagonist with **Tactical Advantage**, see p 16) possesses multiple means of attack, they can inflict damage on more than one opponent who fails to defend.

To keep track, it would be useful to assign tokens to an antagonist to show how many times it might inflict damage.

Every time an Investigator faces off against an antagonist and rolls a Save, mark off or discard an attack. If the Save succeeds, the Investigator inflicts damage. If the Save fails, the creature inflicts the damage noted for the attack used.

After all the Investigators have taken their action in a Moment, any attacks that remain will target the survivors. In this case, the Investigators need to roll their **Saves** solely to defend against the potential harm.

As most Investigators can only make one attack per Moment, they can only hope to fend off any extra attacks from an antagonist with many spare. An Investigator can only hope to hurt an opponent in retaliation if they have not already attacked themselves or taken any other Basic Action.

(Exceptions may arise from possession of a Special Ability, Mythos Magic incantation, artefact or some other mechanic-bending effect.)

Mythos 101

The Dark Universe Yawns Wide

For those less familiar with Lovecraft's stories, he was an author first and foremost. He had no grand plan or wider intentions beyond writing his stories and having them published. Only later has the structure of the Mythos become a thing, mostly through the intervention of others.

The more nebulous and alien your take on Lovecraft the better. In running games with a Lovecraftian edge, you should favour the drama and the inimical forces at work. The Cthulhu Hack presents many minor entities and creatures because those they worship simply defy direct understanding or contact. They shift in alien ways through non-Euclidean dimensions. When glimpsed they shred the human mind by occupying a space in thought and existence at odds with the individual's ability to comprehend.

Lovecraft had half a dozen greater entities at work with their own mass of worshippers and servitors, none of which comfortably fit into standard creature categories. When running The Cthulhu Hack, you can get away with presenting the setting without absolute consistency or true comprehension; Lovecraft never did. Vary the form and action of every antagonist. If you picked a hundred people off the street right now and categorized them, you would probably end up with dozens of potential groupings, none particular, even, or absolute.

Why should creatures of the Lovecraftian pantheon be anything different?

At the top of the scale you have Azathoth and Yog-Sothoth, cosmic entities that conform to concepts and are beyond mere description. If it makes it easier imagine Azathoth as a chaotic mess of strange angles and synesthetic feedback at the dark and twisted centre of the universe, and Yog-Sothoth as an existential foam smeared between and across the dimensions beyond our own.

Shub-Niggurath is either their mother or one of their wives, though neither description matters. Undulating and hideously copious in her presence, she births impossible young who feed upon her and upon reality itself, before being folded back into her endless fecundity.

In inappropriately human terms, Nyarlathotep fits the role of a trickster, like Loki or Set, as well as a messenger. Humanity's sense of free will means nothing to those who worship the Black Pharaoh in pursuit of power or, however unwisely, love. Nyarlathotep has a plan or, perhaps, the plan has Nyarlathotep; whatever the relationship, it constantly interferes in the activities of others, from the court of Azathoth down to the desperate schemes of mere mortals.

These Old Ones interact with mortals in the same way that storms or black holes do - their existence impacts humanity as a peripheral aftershock of their passing. The Old Ones writhe, blind and mindless, somewhere out in the trackless void between worlds. Those who choose to worship them tend to layer their own beliefs and desires around the purpose of their existence - guided, in part, by their greater priesthood.

Like the head of a mortal religion, Cthulhu functions as both a priest and preacher of the Old Ones, as a focus of veneration himself.

Communicating through fevered dreams and prophetic nightmare, Cthulhu lies sleeping, possibly somewhere beneath the Pacific Ocean, in the impossibly twisted city of R'lyeh, waiting for the stars to come right.

Paragraphs of terrible significance in strange book; later unable to find and verify text.

Creatures of the Mythos

BYAKHEE | HD 4 (16 hp), 2 AP ● Claw (2) x 2, Bite (2). If both Claws hit, also Rend (3). If defence fumbles, also Drop (6).

Byakhee appear as a cross between a star-nosed mole, a vampire bat, a grizzly bear, a vulture, a horse, and a zombified primate. They can fly through any medium – air, sea, or even the vacuum of space – with equal dexterity and survival. Often summoned as mounts, they travel through dimensional space with their own purpose when not bound. Survival of riders depends on their own preparation; Byakhee have no heed for the well-being of those who travel on their back.

DEEP ONE | HD 2+ (8+ hp), (HD +2) AP ● Claw (HD +1) x 2. Disadvantage to defend against while submerged. Liquify and mould metal with hands. Amphibious.

Ancient oceanic precedents to humankind; a race of explorers and conquerors in ageless torpor beneath the oceans. Intent upon spreading their adaptable genetic mark through subjugation and enslavement, they can blend their DNA with any species. Perhaps the source of myths about changelings, their hybrid progeny become evident at adolescence. Sentient, but violently xenophobic.

DHOLE | HD 8 (36 hp), 8 AP ● Bite (8). If defence fails by 4+, Swallow (6 / Moment), fight at Disadvantage to escape. All: DEX Save at start of each Moment, else Tremor (Fall Prone). Immunity vs fire.

Massive and monstrous entities, part-leech, part-mole; Dhole have a natural talent to burrow through everything, not least the fabric of reality or dream stuff. Our world seems anathema to the heightened sentience seen in their presence elsewhere, reducing them to thrashing mindless entities when summoned or lured into our world.

DIMENSIONAL SHAMBLER | HD 5 (20 hp), 4 AP ● Claw (4) x 2. If Sanity fails, WIS Save or suffer Grapple (attack at Disadvantage, Countdown 3 or lost forever in another dimension). Vulnerable only to magic or science capable of rupturing dimensions.

Nauseating hybrid of primate and insect; grey, hairless, with sunken eyes like fading embers. They possess impossibly long limbs extending from a bloated, corpse-like trunk. Shamblers have a tenuous link to all dimensions; their appearance rends the fabric of space and time, overlaying distant vistas. They find subsistence in cognition - those who not only see them but process the impossibility of their existence feed their hunger.

ELDER THING | HD 6 (24 hp), 3 AP ● Tentacle (3) x 4. If two hit the same target, Rend (5). Can cast 1d6 random spells. Flying.

Barrel trunked with sinuous manipulators about the circumference and a multitude of sensory nodes upon their "heads". Elder Things dominated many planets in the past. On Earth, their scientists completed inconceivable works of biological and technological manipulation, culminating in the creation of life that would spell their doom. Arrogant and utterly antagonistic, they expand and war constantly.

GHOUL | HD 2 (8 hp), 1 AP ● Claw (2) x 2, Bite (2). Horrific Visage, unless averting gaze or blind-folded (Disadvantage to act), make WIS Save at the start of each Moment, or suffer Shock.

Ageless denizens of subterranean kingdoms; ghouls lie in torpor, only emerging to seek sustenance. No two ghouls look alike; rarely possessed of any vestige of commonality with humanity, beget from hoary precedents of the homo sapiens. Zealously omnivorous, they feast endlessly on living or dead; their appearance numbing soul and sense alike, allowing them to feed upon acquiescent victims.

GREAT RACE OF YITH | HD 9 (36 hp), 4 AP ● Lightning gun (3), targets anything in Line of Sight. Possess form, Disadvantage in DEX Saves. Can cast 1d3 random spells. Time travel.

Conical time travellers from the distant past with a thirst for knowledge, acquired from body-swapping. Custodians of library-cities hidden between the moments at the start of our universe, they reach out to catalogue all things and all time. The Great Race seek the ultimate answer – the truth of their own destruction and the means to prevent it.

HAUNTER | HD 9 (33 hp), 8 AP ● Skull spindle (9), Acidic (3 per Moment, unless Countdown 3: do nothing except clean off acidic goo), Claw (3) x 3. While unaware of the Haunter's location, all attacks auto-fail. Disadvantage on Saves while invisible but locatable.

Summoned assassin, akin to a vicious and merciless bloodhound, though possessed with the power of short-range flight and gifted with endless patience. They can travel between worlds only as stowaways, their essence attached to extra-dimensional obsidian crystals. Capable of tracking and trailing, a sorcerer can set a Haunter to task with a spell that must include three forms of physical marker (like hair, blood, nail clippings, or tears).

MI-GO | HD 3 (12 hp), 3 AP ● Mist projector (6, cold) targets up to Distant range. 3 Spells (GM's choice). Flying.

Hoarders of artefacts and technology; utterly alien of aspect, with no vestige of humanity. Possession means everything to them. When they find technology or resources, they exploit enslave local populations to aid acquisition. Mi-Go engage in foul and ghoulish experimentation on their captives.

NIGHTGAUNT | HD 5 (20 hp), 4 AP ● Sting (3), Horns (3). Any single target who fails to attack, STR Save (Carried, Disadvantage to act). Will drop anyone who struggles, causing (2 x Moments since hold started) in damage from falling. Flying.

Shadow-coloured entities of glistening membrane and sinew, with horned heads, smooth and otherwise without feature. At the beck of spell or mastery, they serve as unquestioning guardians

RHAN-TEGOTH | HD 7 (28 hp), 6 AP ● Slam (8), Claw (4) x 6. If two Claws hit the same target, Vampiric Clutch (CON Save or act at Disadvantage).

A repulsive, globular monstrosity, covered with a million hair-like tentacles tipped with suckers like blind snake heads. Three eye-like tumours swim lazily about its gelatinous bulk, that noisome flesh broken by the sprouting of six sinuous limbs ending in grasping paws tipped with snapping, crab-like claws. A gate-keeper of sorts and likely an offspring of Shub-Niggurath, Its gratitude for servitude and sacrifice comes in access to other worlds and the visitation of other terrible things.

REANIMATED | HD 1-3 (4-12 hp), (HD +2) AP ● Anyone defending against them has Advantage, due to slow movement. Immunity vs pain, charm, hypnotism.

Often found as minions and servants to those who practice the Dark Arts, though they might equally arise from the abuse of technology or drugs. Certain ceremonies and hoary rituals are said to raise them from the essential salts constituent of their living form; else, others might spring up from the leaden repose of carcasses given semblance of vitality through chemicals and driven by fractured memories and a longing for living flesh.

SHOGGOTH | HD 12 (48 hp), 8 AP ● Crush (18) vs 4 nearby targets; DEX Save for half damage. Suffers minimum damage from all attacks. Immunity vs fire, water, electricity, poison, cold. Amphibious.

Dreadnought, soldier and servitor of the Elder Thing, the Shoggoth adopts, adapts and overcomes all obstacles in time, evolving moment by moment. Amorphous and plastic in form, the appearance of Shoggoth might have given rise ancient tales of wizards raising elementals as servants of their will. In all possibility, the finest achievement and the greatest mistake of the Elder Thing's reign.

Special Note

Size Matters: The variable scale of some creatures means that their attacks and defences depend on their size. Any creature may indicate (HD +X), meaning that value is equal to the Hit Dice of the entity adjusted by the modifier shown. For example, a HD 5 Deep One inflicts 6 points of Claw damage.

Alien Weapons: Some entities carry weapons, devices with an unsettling alien appearance, strewn with nodules and flesh-like flaps.

Anyone else might pick up and use one, with a 50-50 chance of success – roll 1 or 2 on d4. Such weapons have a 1D8 Supply Die in the hands of an Investigator.

Spells: While not specified, any creature might know a Spell; the GM should select anything appropriate.

Mythos Magic

The Mythos manifest abilities that warp and rend reality. To humanity, this appears like magic – though it might be impossibly advanced technology at work. Some study this magic, attempting to codify it in formula or ritual.

Investigator will rarely use magic, as the alien concepts fracture the human mind. While knowing a spell, an Investigator steps down their Sanity by one. Unlearning a spell requires therapy, heavy medication, or surgery – but it will restore the lost die. In a

long running game, removing a spell means the character disappears for a time - say the length of a single adventure.

Casting a spell requires an action, normally taking just a moment, and forces a Sanity roll. Antagonists with spells can cast them by giving up an attack. If they have multiple attacks, they do both. They do not lose Sanity.

Example Spells

- **Charm of the Great Deceiver:** Advantage on next Save against any human protagonist.
- **Decay:** Causes all food and drink Nearby to perish or become nauseating.
- **Starry Ward:** Gain 2 AP for a Minute.
- **Sleep:** Forces 4d6 HD of creatures to INT Save or sleep for 2d4 hours.
- **Call the Void:** Create a sphere of absolute darkness around a spot or object, extending to Nearby. Lasts for an hour.
- **Enchantment of Ephraim:** Silence a Nearby target. Empowers caster to speak with their voice. Lasts for an Hour.
- **Gaze of the Three-Lobed Eye:** Traps a Nearby area, stopping movement. Make a CHA Save to escape the entrapment. On a success, release takes a Minute, on a fail release takes at least an

Hour - or enough to generate genuine disadvantage.

- **The Voorish Sign:** Tell whether an action will be a good or bad idea with a cryptic glimpse of possible futures (GM must respond as honestly as possible).
- **Wrath of the Old Ones:** 1d4 creatures in Nearby area sustain 1d12 damage. Neither Armour nor Cover protect from this harm.
- **Puppet of the Pharaoh:** Create an utterly dependent zombie from an intact corpse. HD 2 max.
- **Powder of Ibn-Ghazi:** See anything invisible Nearby. Lasts for 1 Minute.
- **Part the Veil:** Ask a Nearby corpse three questions, to which they respond with the perceived truth.
- **Derange:** 2d6 Nearby targets immediately make a Reaction roll.
- **The Touch of the Silver Key:** Teleport a target to a random Distant location. Roll 1d8 to determine direction and 1d100+100 for distance (in feet).
- **Loathing:** 2d3 targets in Nearby area suffer Disadvantage on all Saves. Lasts for 1 Minute.
- **Elder Sign:** Freeze a single monster in place, unable to act or move. Each turn roll 1d6, 1 or 2 the creature breaks the Sign's ward effect.
- **Reanimation:** Restore a deceased character to life. The dead must

have been deceased for a period no greater than 2d6 days. Reduce all Saves of the reanimated character by 1 point.

- **Teleportation:** Transport a Nearby target to any space known by the caster with an angle sharper than 120°.
- **Invisible Stalker:** Summons an extra-dimensional monster [HD 8, AP 2, Claw (4) x 2, Disadvantage to attack while unseen] to perform one task, including, if wished, the hunting of a meticulously specified target.
- **From Beyond:** Summon 2d4 semi-corporeal, hungry entities (Flying, 1 HD each) with simple intelligence and simpler drives. Lasts for 10 mins.
- **Soul Incision:** Acquire the physical form of a HD 5 creature, while retaining intellectual capacity. Advantage on all physical Saves and Armour Points + 4. Lasts for 1 hour.
- **Maw of Yog-Sothoth:** Stops time completely in a Nearby area. Lasts for 1d4+1 Moments.
- **Call Winged Horror:** Summons a servitor to recover a Distant object or person.
- **Footfalls of the Old Ones.** WIS Save for all Nearby creatures (or roll Upper Hand for creatures) Those who fail must make an immediate roll on the Out of Action table.

Save Innsmouth

A Modern Day Adventure

Introduction

I wrote **Save Innsmouth** as a way to introduce new players to the mechanics of **The Cthulhu Hack** and the brutal truth of the Mythos; that protagonists rarely survive and those who do emerge changed. Minds and bodies break all too easily in the path of churning monsters and the machinations of their masters.

The adventure can be run, including the introduction to the system, in the space of 2-hours - something I managed at Gen Con in 2017. It can become a bit of a helter-skelter ride toward certain doom and revelation. Or, you can play it out as something more stately and considered, akin to the long ruminations of more thoughtful heroes in Lovecraft's stories.

Written as a demo or con game, it requires preparation and confidence from the Gamemaster. If you have only 2-hours, go in fast and enter the events in-media-res, waking the Investigators at the bottom of the pit with hazy memories. From there, overwhelm their senses, challenge their relationships, and use tropes to lure them into poor choices.

If you have 3 - 4 hours, play out the trip on the bus, from Ipswich to Falcon Point. Use the trip across the peninsula to introduce relationships, and layer in the background exposition as hints and clues.

Save Innsmouth is Chapter Zero of a bigger campaign, one that recounts the return of an ancient civilisation. Check out www.healthy-in.com.

Background

"They had talked about dying and half-deserted Innsmouth for nearly a century, and nothing new could be wilder or more hideous than what they had whispered and hinted years before."
--- The Shadow Over Innsmouth

In the last days of winter, 1928, the FBI made numerous arrests in the battle against widespread violation of Prohibition in the seaport of Innsmouth. A massive criminal operation working out of derelict houses and brooding warehouses on the waterfront, the FBI not only completed dozens of arrests, but also dynamited most of the properties.

A decaying vestige of a bygone age, Innsmouth never recovered from the federal intervention. Over the course of almost 80 years, the settlement decayed away to almost nothing.

In mid-2005, Pine Reach Renewal Holdings, an initiative backed by several speculative investors and developers supporting regeneration in Massachusetts and the whole of New England, purchased the town. Alas, PRR Holdings went bankrupt in late 2008, caught in the collapse of the housing bubble. Work stopped and now Innsmouth stands depopulated and derelict. Local news outlets suggest that a buyer has secured tentative rights for a 'Healthy In...'

Dreamer's nightmares given form in other dimension; others blunder in. Alliance sought?

sports and spa village with plans to raze the entire site.

For that very reason, a small group of students come to Innsmouth to capture pictures and video recordings of this last bastion of a bygone America.

The Truth

The close association between the humans and Deep Ones at Innsmouth ended when the Bureau raided the town. The hybrid prisoners taken were stowed away in military prisons and research facilities, never to see the light of day again. The torpedoing of Devil's Reef caused minor damage to the cyclopean city of **Y'ha-nthlei**. The Deep Ones withdrew. If immortality gifted the creatures with anything, it was patience.

Not all inhabitants of Y'ha-nthlei fled. A few Deep Ones remained in tunnels beneath Innsmouth. However, they did not survive long as robbed of support and stripped of numbers they fell afoul of one of their own servitors, the Saltwater Shoggoth. After almost

a century, the Deep Ones have yet to return, but hunger abides...

Not all the Deep One hybrids died in prison or under the scalpel of curious military scientists. **Abiah Debden** is a desperate hybrid that feels the call but knows that something is wrong. He returned to Innsmouth, but couldn't find the answers he sought. He did sense something, a call from beneath the shattered remains of the town; something old and hungry persisted - and he feared it. Believing it to be an avatar of Dagon, and the only link to his heritage, he waylays hikers and sacrifices them.

The Setup

This adventure is all about survival. You should emphasize:

- Resource management, as the investigators start with almost nothing of value and they're forced to depend on each other and what they can scavenge; and,
- The race against time, as the investigators discover the caverns they're trapped in will flood completely. Ten minutes before the

Relighting the Beacon

"...a vast series of raids and arrests occurred, followed by the deliberate burning..."
The Shadow over Innsmouth

While the scattered and sensationalist newspaper reports noted the FBI destroyed swathes of the moldering coastal town, a few stories persist of a stranger fire that burned. If any agents kept personal record, it might hint at the queer, heatless fire that raged and consumed as the FBI pulled back; a flame that continues to burn.

Manuscript cited as too terrible to read - someone reads and is found dead. Text gone.

end of your game session, the tide comes in and any characters still inside the caves will either drown or become easy fodder for the Shoggoth.

The characters involved in this adventure are students, equipped with a few items of gear suitable for a day's hiking and the paraphernalia suited to their purpose in travelling to Innsmouth. Allow them to have whatever they want if it seems sensible to bring it along on a long and tiresome hike through overgrown wilderness and sodden marshland.

Creating Characters

Set the scene, outlined below; then have the Players generate their characters. Pose the listed questions to round out their setup, motivations and background.

"You're all students at Arkham's renowned Miskatonic University. Between terms, you're taking the opportunity to go hiking. You've taken an interest in newspaper and local TV reports of construction in the north-east, along the coast, that will see a piece of history, a town preserved since Prohibition times, bulldozed to make way for a luxury health spa resort. This will be the last chance to see the place intact before The Man clears away another chunk of America's heritage in the name of progress."

- What are you studying at Miskatonic University?
- Why does this trip matter to you?
- What did (the character on your left) do that means you trust them implicitly?
- What little luxury have you allowed yourself, along with your camping gear and hiking kit?

If you want to mix that third question up a bit, write numbers down on a piece of paper equal to the number of players. Go around the table and number the players, starting from your left. Tear the paper up and let the players choose at random. The player trusts the person whose number they just picked. If they picked their own number, have them explain a positive reason why they have chosen to come on this trip despite not trusting anyone here.

The Start

The characters wake, pain stabbing like an insistent alarm clock inside their heads. The stench of brine and rotten fish fills the air and all characters should deduct 3 hit points immediately as they have fallen a good distance on to jagged debris. Warm blood oozes from torn flesh and pools in the mud; the sharp salt tang catches in their throat.

The characters are together at the bottom of a hole in the collapsed

Lost wintry day - slept through; experienced through sensation, strange detail 20 years later.

remains of a crumbling brickwork cellar with only one unblocked exit. Twenty feet above, a jagged hole provides a weak light, loose canvas snaps in the wind. A wracking, painful cough sounds from above, clear over the background noise.

What They Know

Ask what the players want to do. Fill in the details about their surroundings. If they ask why they're here, fill in some of the gaps with information from the Background. Be as vague as you like – they're panicked and hurt.

Other information may need an **Investigation** roll. Use the following detail to either create earlier parts of the adventure or back-up the events when starting later in media res.

- The Investigators have all travelled up from Miskatonic University in Arkham, riding the main bus toward Newburyport in the north. The Investigators wanted to get to Innsmouth, but no Ipswich bus service travels closer than Falcon Point.
- Innsmouth is a building site and best avoided. Some tycoon has made tender on the entire site to build a health spa or something.
- Innsmouth has lain abandoned since the FBI raided the place during Prohibition and razed half the waterfront to the ground.
- The bus journey from Ipswich to Falcon Point does not have any other passengers; the driver seems

disappointed - if not outright upset - that he got any fares at all.
- [**Flashlight**] spots a billboard in Falcon Point with an artist's impression of the 'Healthy In…' sports and spa village. The Dunold Group are behind the development, owned by tycoon Pat Dunold.
- Travel between Falcon Point and Innsmouth necessitates a hike along a narrow tidal road. Residents in the Falcon Point warn against a trip to the ruins of Innsmouth. They suggest better walks along the cliffs toward Essex Bay, to the southeast; they press faded tourist information maps in evidence, showing sun-drenched views and beaches.
- [**Smokes**] A word with leery locals at The Castle bar notes that occasional hikers have headed up the coast, despite advice; they clearly didn't care for the advice either and never chose to return to Falcon Point.
- Beyond the tidal path, the countryside becomes grey and sickly, with leafless trees grasping skyward amidst dunes of straggly grass and sand.
- [**Flashlight**] notes of lack of any animals - not even rats or gulls, in Innsmouth or the surrounding countryside.
- Closer to Innsmouth the dunes give way to the skeletal remains of old farms and occasional abandoned construction equipment. Signs hung on damaged fence work display the sun-faded logo for PRR Holdings, based out of Boston.
- Within Innsmouth, skeletal buildings provide a snapshot of 1920s America, with homes, schools, stores, and the fire blackened remains of a single church. Close to the centre of town,

Black winged thing flies into house at night; cannot be found or identified. Developments ensue.

there's an abandoned portable cabin emblazoned with a PPR Holdings logo.

- At any point within sight of the town, the Investigators may see something like looks like a bonfire or beacon. A <u>failed</u> **WIS Save** means the character discounts the vision as a trick of the sunlight playing off shattered glass. A successful **WIS Save** requires that the Investigator roll [**Sanity**] as they realise they can see the odd flame <u>through</u> the trees and buildings. On Investigators get closer to the centre of town, finding the flame becomes like seeking the end of a rainbow.
- A bridge across a narrow, debris-choked river leads into a semi-circular square at the centre of the town. On the right-hand side, a tall, cupola-crowned building with remnants of yellow paint and a half-effaced sign announce the 'Gilman House', a once grand hotel and soon to be the site of the central resort complex. The building should entice Investigators to further investigation, although the trap set by the bus driver can appear inside any building. The whispers he hears have told him where to set the trap - this is not a linear adventure, but destiny's path.

Finding specific buildings in town will require an Investigation roll with the possibility of garnering antiquated household goods or possessions. Determined characters can find a Revolver (**Supply Die 1d6**) or kitchen Knife. Later, in the caves, investigation can uncover discarded camping gear, which will include items suitable as improvised weapons, including a Flare Gun (**Supply Die 1d4**).

What Next?

If the characters cry out for help, someone shuffles close to the edge of the hole above, sending bit of debris down in a dusty shower.

After a bout of phlegm-filled, chest-wracking coughs, a shadow looms in the half-light - the bus driver. He appears sad, his oddly staring eyes reflective.

If the characters attempt conversation or plead for assistance, he gazes back, sullen faced. Tears drip from his fleshy cheeks. In a barely audible whisper, almost apologetic, he says, '**Tradition is a powerful thing.**' With that, he moves back from the edge and, with a thunderous crash, something heavy falls across the hole and cuts out the light.

The Tunnels

Once the characters get their bearings they will find a debris-strewn passageway leading out of the rough brick-walled cellar. The hole above has been sealed with a slab of something immensely heavy - metal or concrete - and no amount of effort will shift it, even if the characters could work out a way to reach it together.

Labyrinthine passages honeycomb the soft rock beneath Innsmouth; they echo with the distant thunder of the waves and an occasional distant bark, presumably of escaping subterranean gas. Surfaces within the passage display irregular shifts in level and angle with prodigious steps and drops, demanding constant concentration while moving to stop slips or falls.

Passages and chambers intersect, suggesting seawater erosion, but close inspection shows evidence of careful artisanship. There's something deeply unhuman about the shapes and scouring in the stone; the dimensions and decorations offer clear signs of some blasphemous artifice.

The carving displays a grotesque and repulsive design, conveying a story of a malign and repugnant nature. Anyone studying the designs at length needs to make a **WIS Save**.

If they fail, they make no revelations, not fully grasping the twisting swirls of primitive patterns.

With a success, the player must roll [**Sanity**]. The wall carvings present a complex vision, multi-layered and stretched across many surfaces. Seen from the right (or perhaps wrong) angle, the images suggest artifice by something in possession of unhuman senses. The patterns convey images of savage sacrifice and inter-species union in the name of monstrous entities that dwarf anything known by humanity. The configuration of characters suggests that the humans

engaged willingly in these obscene acts.

An **Investigation** roll recalls a visit to the Museum of Miskatonic University in Arkham. The carvings mirror the elaborate workmanship seen on jewellery rescued from deep coastal waters and now held in permanent exhibit within the museum. Rumoured by locals to come from the wreck of a pirate ship, analysis has found no comparison to the artisanship of any civilisation in any recorded period.

[**Flashlight**] notes that in most passages and chambers floor and ceiling appear polished and smooth. Any detritus or debris lies close to the walls, as if pushed aside - perhaps by the passage of water flowing in and out of the chamber.

Further inspection [**Flashlight**] reveals a clear variation in the age of the carvings. The clarity and precision of the shapes and evidence of erosion suggest work ranging from centuries old to as recent as just years - perhaps even months.

Listed below are the various points of interest within the caverns and some of the possible encounters that await the characters. Reinforce that all chambers (unless noted) show obvious signs of a high-water mark at ceiling height. A detritus of smooth stones, shells, seaweed, and coarse-grained

Fog or smoke; assumes shape under incantations.

pale sand litters the ground everywhere, with occasional junk.

At some point during their investigation of the tidal chambers, the characters will notice (without need for a roll) that the intermittent background croaking has stopped. At this point, you might give pause and ask what the players want to do next, having described their environment and options. Give them a moment to respond, and then cut them off mid-sentence with a batrachian scream!

You might want to practice and research an appropriate approach to making this sound. I recommend finding a Screaming Toad video on You Tube as a solid starting point. Failing that, a well-prepared sound clip through a speaker should suffice.

Busman's Sacrifice

A rough chamber accessed through a hole halfway up the wall at the end of a passage; carpeted with fish scales, lumps of stone and scattered litter. Close inspection finds the yellow-white litter is light and porous. Make a **WIS Save**. On success, roll [**Sanity**] as the character recognises the granular detritus as shattered bone.

On a failed **WIS Save**, the characters find an intact human vertebra and several teeth amongst the waste, at which point each must succeed in a

CON Save or become nauseous (Disadvantage on all rolls for 1D6 Minutes); but they don't make the connection to the body gravel.

Feeding Place

There is a dead body here, left behind by the Shoggoth. Given the remains look like a particularly gross display of explosive decompression and several elements appear missing or ground to paste, roll [**Sanity**]. [**Flashlight**] reveals something of immediate use that a hiker might reasonably carry, like a torch, spare batteries, a first aid kit, or a cell phone. A gore-stained canvas wallet contains several dollar bills, an ID card and a bus ticket.

Mating Cell

Small cells containing smooth flat boulders. Each has two pair of well-worn depressions, front and back, and the fragile remains of metal manacles. The elaborate carvings around the walls provide explicit record of the monstrous activities acted upon those held in these chambers by the Deep Ones, requiring a Sanity roll.

Toad Colony

Grey-skinned toads, with pale, sightless eyes, nest across the floor. In repose, gentle croaking ripples across the room. Careful steps, and a **DEX**

Save (or cunning plan), will get the characters across without disturbing the nest. Failure disturbs, or kills, one or more toads setting off an echoing cacophony of guttural screams, certain to draw the attention of the Shoggoth. Ask what the players want to do, pressure a response - then decide what happens next.

Flooded Cave

The passage descends into dark, swirling waters, with no alternative means to progress other than retreat. Characters need to make a **STR Save** <u>and</u> a **CON Save**. If they fail the first, they cannot swim with sufficient power to progress beyond the barrier. They end in the original chamber and suffer Disadvantage on **STR Saves** for the remainder of the Scene. If they succeed on the STR, but fail the **CON Save**, they reach the other side, but hurt themselves in the process, suffering 1d4hp in damage. Blood in the water will attract the Shoggoth - if you're Mapping the Caves, roll the Resource Die; otherwise, rolling 1 on 1d6 means unwelcome news.

Saltwater Shoggoth

The Shoggoth is a pale grey-blue monstrosity of ever-shifting form; sinuous tentacles, unhuman eyes, and the occasional grasping limbs or screaming mouths of past victims. A character struck by the Saltwater Shoggoth must make a **CON Save** or start to drown, suffering Disadvantage on all actions unless someone pulls them free by forfeiting an action.

The best tactic is to avoid the Shoggoth altogether. The GM should avoid all-out attacks, as they are certain to be fatal. Hit-and-run strikes should suffice – a tense moment when a tentacle grasps a trailing limb through a narrow gap or something brushes a swimmer from under the water's surface. A glancing blow can disable, utterly shattering bones or yanking limbs off. Best to run!

Resolution

The adventure's conclusion depends on the actions of the fate of the characters.

The least ideal - have the camera view sweep out to a cave pocked coastline, with crashing waves and the brooding ruins of Innsmouth. A human scream abruptly cut off by a batrachian bellow.

The ideal resolution would be for the characters to escape with their lives, battered, sore, and traumatized. Ask the players what the characters do in the weeks and months that follow. If construction progresses, you play out the scene as above; just swap out the ruins of Innsmouth for a luxury resort spa.

Hideous world superimposed on visible world; akin to distortion of light or mass hallucination.

Example of Play

While following up on a lead from the customs office about illegal shipments into a private warehouse, the investigators Doctor Allen Farthing, adventurer Victoria Covey and archivist Marcus Palmer have gone to snoop around. Outside, they find a cargo crate covered with a tarpaulin.

MARCUS: Can I have a look around the grounds of the place?

GM: What are you looking for?

MARCUS: Anything. Footprints, probably.

GM: Sure. You find a trail of dark staining across the cobbles of the yard around the warehouse, leading from the covered crate toward the main truck access into building. Roll your Flashlights.

MARCUS rolls 2 on a D8, noting reduction to a D6

GM: You get some of the blood on your clothes. You're not sure whether it's fresh or if the recent rain fall might have loosened old blood on the stones.

VICTORIA: I'm going over to the tarp. I'm going to pull it back to check into the crate.

GM: When you pull back the tarp, the stench of blood and urine hits you immediately. A mangled and twisted corpse, glistening with half-dried blood lies inside, partially clothed. Roll your Sanity.

VICTORIA rolls 3 on a D10

VICTORIA: Revolted, but in control, I fold the tarp back and step away. I wave an arm toward the others warning them not to look. "They killed someone. Brutal. Horrible. Just don't look…"

ALLEN: Are you okay?

VICTORIA: Yes. Yes. Just don't.

MARCUS: Okay, so I want to get inside the warehouse. Before we go in, uh, can we tell if there is anyone around?

GM: You can't tell whether the ground floor windows have been painted on the inside or are just dirty; whatever, you can't see in anywhere. However, on the floor above you can see a faint, flickering glimmer - perhaps a flame from an improvised torch or a fire, like in a steel barrel or something. The flicker comes from a window in the north-west corner. Roll your Flashlights.

MARCUS rolls 4 on his D6

MARCUS: Does the flame look normal? I mean, natural? It isn't, like, some flare from some ritual or something.

GM (frowning and shaking his head): No. It looks normal. I mean, perhaps a bit odd to have an open flame in a building, but… (shrugs)

ALLEN: Okay. We find a way inside. Can we use the truck doors? Is there an entrance for workers?

GM: Yeah. There's a door within the door. It's open, just a crack.

VICTORIA: Aren't there any night-watchmen or something? Shouldn't there be a guard?

GM: Have you checked that out? Did you speak to someone?

VICTORIA: Yeah. Allen and I spent some time in local pubs and coffee shops. Should I roll Smokes?

GM: Yeah. You both got the gist that the place had a lot more security than much of the rest of the docks. As well as employing a lot of extra day labour, whoever owns the place hired half a dozen locals to keep an eye on the warehouse day and night.

VICTORIA rolls 1 on a D8, noting a drop to D6.

VICTORIA: Right, we head inside.

GM: As you push the door you hear low voices, muffled.

VICTORIA: Damn. I follow the push with a kick and pull my gun out ready.

GM: You need to make a DEX Save. You push the door and then kick it, so whoever's inside has a chance to react. If you fail, they strike out reflexively as the door moves and harm you before you can arm yourself.

VICTORIA rolls a 16 versus a DEX 11.

GM: A sharp slice from the side of someone's hand sends shooting pains up your arm. Your gun clatters to the floor. You suffer 2 hit points damage.

MARCUS: Seeing the strike from inside, I dive through and hope to catch someone off-guard with a swift hand-to-hand attack.

MARCUS rolls a 20 versus a STR 13, cursing.

GM: No problem. For them, anyway. You misjudge the step through and another assailant barrels into you, knocking you to the ground and the door closed with a sharp clang. Allen, you're outside the door. Marcus, you suffer 2 hit points damage and you're lying flat out on the ground. You can see there are three people here – two men and a woman – all dressed in street clothes but with an odd yellow sash draped over their right shoulder. The sash has symbols on it, but now isn't the time to be reading them.

ALLEN: I try to open the door. (The GM shakes his head.) It's locked. Great. Is there another way inside?

ALLEN rolls a 3 on his D6 Flashlights die.

GM: Sure. You can see a downpipe fixed to the side of the building. You could climb that. On the upper floor, the pipe runs close enough to a window to get inside. It'll take a DEX Save – and if you fail, you fall.

ALLEN rolls a 11 against his DEX 13.

GM: You climb the pipe and reach across to the window. Through the grime-smeared glass you can see half-a-dozen people gathered around what looks like a door. It's freestanding and in its frame – and the orange light spills out from the cracks around the door. The people are chanting, "Wza-y'ei! Wza-y'ei! Y'kaa haa bho–ii, Rhan-Tegoth–Cthulhu fhtagn–" What do you do now?

What Next?

You can find the basic premise of this Example of Play outlined in the demo adventure **Nocturnal Rites**, which you can download for free: http://bit.ly/TCHdemo

Like **Save Innsmouth**, you will find this demo ideal for introducing new players and it can be run in less than an hour. Feel free to expand on the detail and continue the story in your own voice.

The demo also includes a couple of ready-to-play characters. You can also download different versions of the character sheet, for free, from RPGNow and DriveThruRPG: http://bit.ly/TCH5h33t

Beyond the core rules, The Cthulhu Hack offers more guidance and adventures:

From Unformed Realms includes many carefully created random tables designed to create new horrors or transform tired monsters into something fresh.

The Haunter of the Dark provides a guide to digging valuable story-telling gems out of Lovecraft's own tales. It offers guidance on layering investigations and a sequel to "The Haunter of the Dark".

Shapeless living thing forms nucleus at heart of building or settlement; purpose unknown.

Open Gaming Licence

DESIGNATION OF PRODUCT IDENTITY: The following items are hereby identified as Product Identity, as defined in the Open Game License version 1.0a, Section 1(e), and are not Open Content: The Cthulhu Hack logo, The Cthulhu Hack and Just Crunch Games are all trademarks of Paul Baldowski. All trademarks, artwork, logos and layout are product identity. All text not related to game mechanics descriptions is Product Identity, including Mythos 101. Elements specifically in the public domain or previously designated Open Game Content are not included in this declaration.

DESIGNATION OF OPEN GAME CONTENT: Except for material designated as Product Identity, the game mechanics of this product are Open Game Content.

OPEN GAME LICENSE Version 1.0a

The following text is the property of Wizards of the Coast, Inc. and is Copyright 2000 Wizards of the Coast, Inc ("Wizards"). All Rights Reserved.

1. Definitions: (a) "Contributors" means the copyright and/or trademark owners who have contributed Open Game Content; (b) "Derivative Material" means copyrighted material including derivative works and translations (including into other computer languages), potation, modification, correction, addition, extension, upgrade, improvement, compilation, abridgment or other form in which an existing work may be recast, transformed or adapted; (c) "Distribute" means to reproduce, license, rent, lease, sell, broadcast, publicly display, transmit or otherwise distribute; (d)"Open Game Content" means the game mechanic and includes the methods, procedures, processes and routines to the extent such content does not embody the Product Identity and is an enhancement over the prior art and any additional content clearly identified as Open Game Content by the Contributor, and means any work covered by this License, including translations and derivative works under copyright law, but specifically excludes Product Identity. (e) "Product Identity" means product and product line names, logos and identifying marks including trade dress; artefacts; creatures characters; stories, storylines, plots, thematic elements, dialogue, incidents, language, artwork, symbols, designs, depictions, likenesses, formats, poses, concepts, themes and graphic, photographic and other visual or audio representations; names and descriptions of characters, spells, enchantments, personalities, teams, personas, likenesses and special abilities; places, locations, environments, creatures, equipment, magical or supernatural abilities or effects, logos, symbols, or graphic designs; and any other trademark or registered trademark clearly identified as Product identity by the owner of the Product Identity, and which specifically excludes the Open Game Content; (f) "Trademark" means the logos, names, mark, sign, motto, designs that are used by a Contributor to identify itself or its products or the associated products contributed to the Open Game License by the Contributor (g) "Use", "Used" or "Using" means to use, Distribute, copy, edit, format, modify, translate and otherwise create Derivative Material of Open Game Content. (h) "You" or "Your" means the licensee in terms of this agreement.

2. The License: This License applies to any Open Game Content that contains a notice indicating that the Open Game Content may only be Used under and in terms of this License. You must affix such a notice to any Open Game Content that you Use. No terms may be added to or subtracted from this License except as described by the License itself. No other terms or conditions may be applied to any Open Game Content distributed using this License.

3. Offer and Acceptance: By Using the Open Game Content You indicate Your acceptance of the terms of this License.

4. Grant and Consideration: In consideration for agreeing to use this License, the Contributors grant You a perpetual, worldwide, royalty-free, non-exclusive license with the exact terms of this License to Use, the Open Game Content.

5. Representation of Authority to Contribute: If You are contributing original material as Open Game Content, You represent that Your Contributions are Your original creation and/or You have sufficient rights to grant the rights conveyed by this License.

6. Notice of License Copyright: You must update the COPYRIGHT NOTICE portion of this License to include the exact text of the COPYRIGHT NOTICE of any Open Game Content You are copying, modifying or distributing, and You must add the title, the copyright date, and the copyright holder's name to the COPYRIGHT NOTICE of any original Open Game Content you Distribute.

7. Use of Product Identity: You agree not to Use any Product Identity, including as an indication as to compatibility, except as expressly licensed in another, independent Agreement with the owner of each element of that Product Identity. You agree not to indicate compatibility or co-adaptability with any Trademark or Registered Trademark in conjunction with a work containing Open Game Content except as expressly licensed in another, independent Agreement with the owner of such Trademark or Registered Trademark. The use of any Product Identity in Open Game Content does not constitute a challenge to the ownership of that Product Identity. The owner of any Product Identity used in Open Game Content shall retain all rights, title and interest in and to that Product Identity.

8. Identification: If you distribute Open Game Content You must clearly indicate which portions of the work that you are distributing are Open Game Content.

9. Updating the License: Wizards or its designated Agents may publish updated versions of this License. You may use any authorized version of this License to copy, modify and distribute any Open Game Content originally distributed under any version of this License.

10 Copy of this License: You MUST include a copy of this License with every copy of the Open Game Content You Distribute.

11. Use of Contributor Credits: You may not market or advertise the Open Game Content using the name of any Contributor unless You have written permission from the Contributor to do so.

12 Inability to Comply: If it is impossible for You to comply with any of the terms of this License with respect to some or all of the Open Game Content due to statute, judicial order, or governmental regulation then You may not Use any Open Game Material so affected.

13 Termination: This License will terminate automatically if You fail to comply with all terms herein and fail to cure such breach within 30 days of becoming aware of the breach. All sublicenses shall survive the termination of this License.

14. Reformation: If any provision of this License is held to be unenforceable, such provision shall be reformed only to the extent necessary to make it enforceable.

15 COPYRIGHT NOTICE

Open Game License v 1.0 Copyright 2000, Wizards of the Coast, Inc.

THE BLACK HACK, Copyright 2016, Gold Piece Publications; Author: David Black.

ADDITIONAL THINGS, Copyright 2016, Author: David Black

THE CTHULHU HACK, Copyright 2016, Just Crunch Games; Author: Paul Baldowski.

Structure stands by a pool - reflection fixed thro' centuries; mirror reveals state of ruin.

Index

Special beings with special senses from remote universes; visions open across strange vistas.

THE CTHULHU HACK

NAME: _____

OCCUPATION: _____

ARCHETYPE: _____

Strength	Dexterity	Constitution	Wisdom	Intelligence	Charisma
vs Melee attacks Harm that cannot be dodged	vs Ranged attack Harm that can be dodged	vs Poison, disease, pain and instant death	vs Deception, illusion and complexity	vs Puzzles, magic alien science	vs Mind control, hypnosis, glamour
ADVANTAGE	ADVANTAGE	ADVANTAGE	ADVANTAGE	ADVANTAGE	ADVANTAGE

Flashlights Spot, Recall, Research

Smokes Coerce, Carouse, Bully

Sanity

Hit Points

Damage If no dice, Unarmed = 1pt
Armed
Unarmed

Abilities

By night, a structure stands in great magnificence; by day, only abandonment and ruin remain.